What's the Opposite?

A LIFT-THE-FLAP BOOK

For Christopher and Jane

Published by the Penguin Group
Penguin Books Ltd, 27 Wrights Lane, London W8 5TZ, England
Penguin Books USA Inc., 375 Hudson Street, New York, New York 10014, USA
Penguin Books Australia Ltd, Ringwood, Victoria, Australia
Penguin Books Canada Ltd, 10 Alcorn Avenue, Toronto, Ontario, Canada M4V 3B2
Penguin Books (NZ) Ltd, 182–190 Wairau Road, Auckland 10, New Zealand

Penguin Books Ltd, Registered Offices: Harmondsworth, Middlesex, England

First published in Canada by Thomas Allen & Son Ltd 1984
First published in Great Britain by Ventura Publishing Ltd 1984
Published in Puffin Books 1996
1 3 5 7 9 10 8 6 4 2

Made and printed in Singapore by Tien Wah Press (Pte) Ltd

What's the Opposite?

A LIFT-THE-FLAP BOOK

Eric Hill

PUFFIN BOOKS

What is the opposite of
hairy?

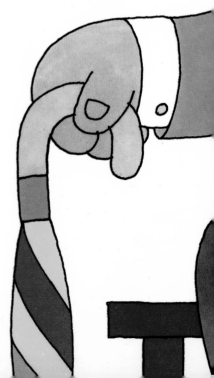

What is the opposite of

dark?

What is the opposite of

easy?

What is the opposite of

new?

What is the opposite of full?

What is the opposite of

closed?

What is the opposite of

above?

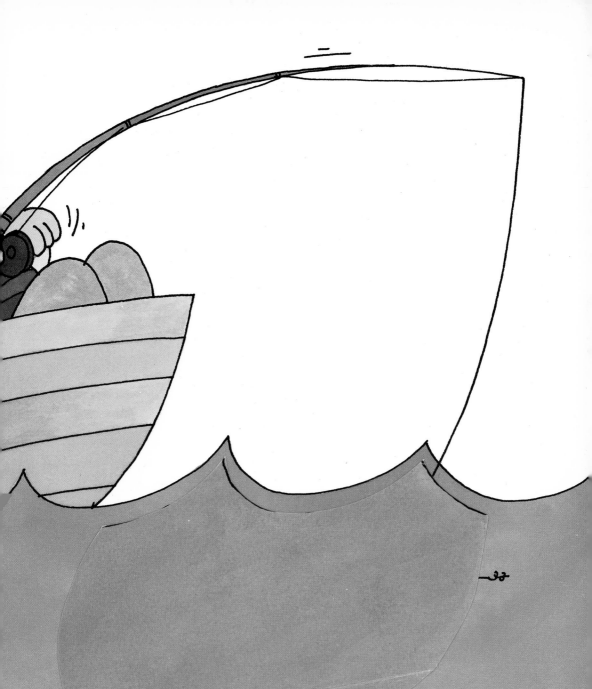

What is the opposite of naughty?

What is the opposite of

dirty ?